incredible
Facts about

koalas

MEGAN MORITA

CONTENT

ADORABLE KOALA

Lovely and fluffy koalas stole people's hearts across the world.

Their big eyes, cuddly appearance and innocent behaviour make koala one of the most adored animals on Earth. Let's reveal more secrets about koalas. Let's find out what koalas like, how they live and how we can save them from extinction.

5

ALL ABOUT KOALA

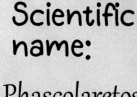

KOALAS AREN'T BEARS!

They are a type of mammal called **marsupials** who give birth to underdeveloped babies.

Baby koala is born blind, earless and deaf to continue growing in a **pouch**.

Koala is Australian's most famous animal.

Scientific name:

Phascolaretos Cinereus

White koala lives only in the wild in Australia on the Southwest and East.

HOW THEY LOOK

Fur color: grey with a cream-coloured chest.
Height: 60-85 cm

Koala's size, color and shape can differ depending on the place they live.
They don't have fur on their palms.

They have 5 fingers which is perfect for climbing the Eucalyptus trees.

Koala is well-known for its large round head, big furry ears and big black nose.

The eucalyptus leaves are low in energy containing only 5 % sugars.

Koalas are vegetarians.
They eat eucalyptus leaves even if it is poisonous to most animals!

They have a fibre digestive organ **caecum** detoxifying the poisonous **cyanide** from the leaves.
Thanks to that they don't have to compete with other animals (except of possun and glidder) for food.

Koala's name in Aboryginal means "no drink" because they get water mostly from leaves and rarely drink water.

Koala mums can give birth to twins but it is rare.

Baby Koala

Baby koala, called **Joey,** grows in his mother's pouch for 6 months. When little koala is born it climbs up to the pouch.

Koala is a foodie! He chooses only the best quality food.

HOW THEY LIVE

Koalas live on **eucalyptus** trees.

They are **nocturnal** animals so they sleep during the day and are mostly active at night.

When they climb they leave characteristic marks/scratches on eucalyptus trees.
The trees shed every year therefore when you look at the tree you can spot if koalas like that tree.

Births take place between November and February.

Koalas live 10–12 years in the wild.

The closest koala's relative is wombat.

save koalas

In February 2012 the koala's status has changed from *vulnerable* to *endangered.*
This status provides them increased level of protection in Australia. That's good news!

About **80 %** koalas perished because of human activities, droughts and bushfires.

Koalas are also losing space to live because of excessive tree-clearing. When the eucalyptus trees are disappearing they have nowhere to go.

Koalas are totally unique in the animal world. They are the only living members of their family — phascolarctidae.

HOW YOU CAN HELP

You could:

- **adopt** a koala
- **inform** others about koala extinction
- sign up or create your own **petition** to save koalas
- **donate** to a koala conservation charity
- make a **poster** about koala saving
- **plant** eucalpytus trees in Australia
- **teach** adults to stop using toxic garden sprays as pesticides and creosote as koalas sometimes eat soil
- **visualize** that in the future koalas still exist and how happy you are about it
- write a **letter** to politicians asking them to take action to save koalas
- **never make koala stressed** because stressed koala can get sick easily

Hi!

MORE FACTS

• They stick to their home ranges. Respect for the boundaries of another koala's territory
is one of the most important principles in the koala's codex.

• They have poor vision but other senses stronger. Especially hearing!

• Females usually have white chest and a pouch. Males are bigger and have a bigger black nose.

• Because the eucalyptus leaves are low in energy koalas need to
sleep for many hours.

CUTE ANIMALS

We all know that koalas are super cute but there are so many more!
Here is a few examples of cute animals.
Do you agree with our choices?
Would you add another species to this list?

RED PANDA
Fluffy fur, adorable eyes, innocent look. This animal has all the necessary features to be called one of the world's cutest animals.
Red pandas live in the Eastern Himalayas and South-western China.

LEAFY SEA DRAGON

They're related to sea Horses and live off the coast of South and East Australia.
They slurp up their food with their long snout as if they were using a drinking straw.

EMPEROR TAMARIN

They live in groups of two to 15 animals in the rainforest in Brasil, Peru and Bolivia. They eat fruit, flowers, nectar, gum, and small animals. Very often they give birth to twins.

QUOKKA

Why are they so cute?
Because they smile!
They can only be found mostly
on Rottnest Island and Bald
Island in Australia.
They love to climb small trees
and shrubs in search of their
next meal, and to rest.

FENNEC FOX

Their long ears allow them
to regulate their body
temperature in the hot dessert.
These foxes are nocturnal
animals.They hide from heat in
sand burrows during the day.
They live in North Africa and
Asia, Arid desert regions.

WOMBAT

They are the second largest of all marsupials living Wombats. They can run as fast as a human.
When a predator is close they dive down their burrows and block off the entrance with their butts.

HEDGEHOG

He can curl up into a spiky ball when predators such as badgers are around. They eat berries and fruits but the staple of their diet is made up from pests such as beetles and caterpillars.

RACCOON DOG

Hey live in forests, wetlands, farmlands, and urban areas from Sweden to Japan. They hibernate in winter. They don't bark but give off a high-pitched whine

ARCTIC FOX

They can be found in arctic tundra in Canada to Russia, Europe, Greenland, and Iceland. They can eat almost anything. Even fruits!
In the summer months they hide extra food under rocks for winter.

MEERKAT

They have dark patches around their eyes to cut down glare from the sun and help them see far into the distance. Meerkats live in all kinds of deserts. They are immune to snake's venom.

PANDA

They can swim and climb trees. Pandas spend 10-16 hours a day feeding, mainly on bamboo. Sometimes they also eat bamboo roots, stems, shoots, leaves or eggs. Baby pandas are born pink!

Hi there!

I hope you enjoyed the experience with my book.

Please leave your review.
That means the world to me!

Check the Author Page to discover more inspiring books:

Made in the USA
Middletown, DE
23 August 2023

37238045R00018